THE TREATY OF VERSAILLES

The Treaty that Marked the End of World War I

Written by Jonathan D'Haese
In collaboration with Thomas Jacquemin
Translated by Jessica Foster

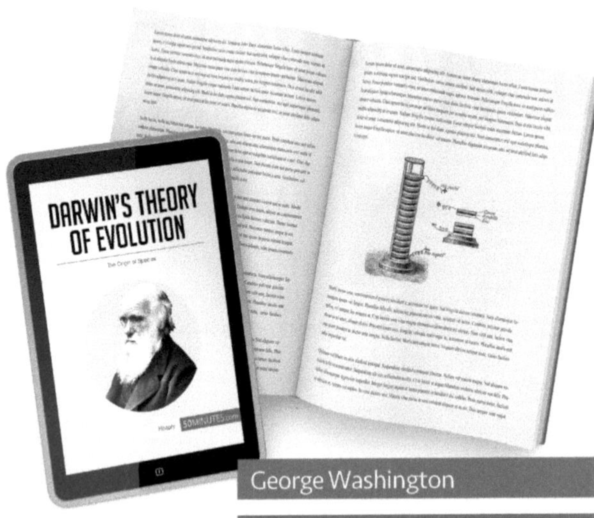

THE TREATY OF VERSAILLES

KEY INFORMATION

- **When:** 18 January 1919 – 10 January 1920.
- **Where:** Paris.
- **Context:**
  - End of World War I (1914-1918).
  - The signing of the Armistice (11 November 1918).
- **Key protagonists:**
  - Georges Clemenceau, French Prime Minister (1841-1929).
  - Thomas Woodrow Wilson, US President (1856-1924).
  - Vittorio Orlando, Italian Prime Minister (1860-1952).
  - David Lloyd George, British Prime Minister (1863-1945).
- **Impact:**
  - The creation of the League of Nations in 1919.
  - Rivalry between the European Allies.
  - The weakening of the great Western powers.
  - The rise of nationalism.

INTRODUCTION

The Treaty of Versailles marked the end of the First World War between Germany and the Allies, represented by Georges Clemenceau (France), David Lloyd George (Great Britain), Woodrow Wilson (United States) and Vittorio Orlando (Italy). It was signed on 28 June 1919 in the Hall of Mirrors at the Palace of Versailles, the same place where the proclamation of the German Empire had taken place in 1871. By imposing this location on Germany, France wanted to symbolically rid itself of the humiliation endured during the Franco-Prussian War in 1870 by forcing Germany to recognise its responsibilities in the world war.

The terms of the treaty were severe towards the defeated country. An eighth of Germany's territory was annexed and they were forced to give up their colonies to the victors. In addition, they had to give Alsace-Lorraine back to France and pay a heavy fine for damages caused during the war. The treaty also stipulated the abolition of military service, reducing the German army to 100 000 men, in the aim of limiting its power. In order to ensure that the many terms were respected, the Allies planned to occupy the left bank of the Rhine for 15 years.

The German delegates eventually signed the document, which was viewed in Berlin as a humiliating and hostile diktat imposed by the victors. In the end, the treaty was a diplomatic failure. It stirred up rivalries among European powers, anxious to maintain their standing, to the detriment of a damaged Germany, where the seeds of the Second World War were already being sown.

CONTEXT

EUROPE UNDER GERMAN DOMINATION

Assassination of Archduke Franz Ferdinand of Austria.

On 28 June 1914, Archduke Franz Ferdinand of Austria (1863-1914) and his wife were shot by the Serb anarchist Gavrilo Princip (1894-1918) in Sarajevo. The European states used this pretext to declare war on each other. On 4 August 1914, the German general Helmuth von Moltke (1848-1916) sent his army towards Paris. He was counting on a quick victory against France, but the resistance mounted by Belgium, then by France, stopped the German advance in its tracks on the banks of the Marne.

The winter of 1914 saw the armies stuck in a war of attrition. For many months, they faced each other on either side of a front line that was over 400 miles long, without any offensive action by either of the warring countries giving an advantage to one side or other. At the beginning of 1918, the situation was critical for the Allies: after four years of fighting, the German Empire dominated Europe, had managed to keep its army intact and had successfully protected its territory from invasion.

On 3 March 1918, the Treaty of Brest-Litovsk (Belarus), a separate peace treaty signed with the Soviets, guaranteed Germany victory in the East. The German general Erich Ludendorff (1865-1937) seized the opportunity to reinforce his troops on the Western front. There he launched three offensives: one in Picardy (21 March), one in Flanders (9 April), then one on the Chemin des Dames (27 May). These operations nearly brought victory to the Germans, who managed to advance 40 miles on the Allied front, reaching Amiens and even threatening Paris in June. However, the resistance mounted by the British and French armies at the Second Battle of the Marne, which lasted from 15 to 20 July 1918, revealed the enemy army's weaknesses and forced them to retreat to the Department of Aisne on 18 July. This was the start of Germany's decline.

THE INTERVENTION OF THE UNITED STATES

President Wilson asking Congress to declare war on Germany.

The US joined the war in April 1917, and President Woodrow Wilson hoped for a quick victory against the Second Reich, without eliminating it completely. On 8 January 1918, he presented his "Fourteen Points" to the United States Congress, which set out the necessary conditions for re-establishing peace among the European states following the war. These included the abolition of secret diplomacy, limits on weaponry and the creation of a League of Nations, tasked with ensuring the territorial integrity and sovereignty of the

European states.

The American president's objective was pragmatic. He wanted to persuade the two blocs of the need to reach a balanced peace agreement without annexation, based on the principle of people's right to self-determination. Initially, the move was a failure. At the beginning of 1918, the military offensives launched in the Somme to destabilise the German front prevented the diplomatic resolution of the conflict. At this stage in the war, Wilson realised that peace was only attainable with the intervention of the American army to allow the balance of power to be reversed in favour of the Allies.

Indeed, after only just managing not to collapse during the German offensives between March and April, the French army had lost all ability to launch major offensives. The position of the British was no more enviable; they were mourning the loss of 236 000 men.

On 26 March 1918, Georges Clemenceau placed the Allied forces situated on the Western front under the sole command of Marshal Ferdinand Foch (1851-1929). On 27 May, the new Allied *generalissimo* contacted John Pershing (1860-1948), commander of the American Expeditionary Force, to convince him to take part in a general offensive against Germany. But Pershing had just arrived in France with an army corps of just 14 500 men. After lengthy negotiations, Congress agreed to send him a million soldiers who had been mobilised by the Selective Service Act, a law that had enabled conscription in the United States since May 1917.

Reassured by the Americans' participation, Foch launched a joint Allied offensive in the Department of the Somme on 8 August 1918. Although only acting as reinforcement, the presence of three million American soldiers in Europe weighed the conflict decisively in favour of the Allies.

APPROACHING THE ARMISTICE

By virtue of now having higher numbers of men and artillery, the British managed to break through German lines in Picardy, Artois and Flanders at the end of September. Now in complete disarray, the Prussians were faced with the collapse of their allies in Eastern Europe.

Forced to retreat on all fronts, General Ludendorff advised Wilhelm II (King of Prussia and German Emperor, 1859-1941) to surrender. On 3 October 1918, the Emperor sent Prince Maximilian of Baden (German politician, 1867-1929) to ask President Wilson for peace.

The Reich thus found itself on the brink of collapse. In Berlin, far-left political factions exploited the population's unhappiness to organise strikes against the "imperialist war" and set up workers' councils (soviets), thus following the example set by the Russian revolutions. Now powerless, Wilhelm II abdicated on 9 November. The next day, the Reichstag (parliamentary assembly of the German Empire) announced it was becoming a Republic. In the meantime, a delegation, led by Matthias Erzberger (German politician, 1875-1921) crossed the French front lines to negotiate the terms of an armistice. The discussions began on 8 November in Marshal Foch's personal train carriage. Taking advantage of the Germans' defeat, the Allied leader imposed surrender with draconian conditions upon them. They had to accept the liberation of Allied prisoners of war and leave territories they had invaded in the West, notably Alsace-Lorraine, within a fortnight.

Signed on 11 November 1918, the Armistice put an end to four years of armed fighting on the European continent. The conditions were then met for the imposition of a peace treaty dominated by France's interests and desires for revenge over a defeated Germany. But the events to come would show that victory does not necessarily guarantee peace.

BIOGRAPHIES

GEORGE CLEMENCEAU, THE FATHER OF FRENCH VICTORY

Georges Clemenceau.

Born in 1841, Georges Clemenceau was the head of the radical left before 1914. When France went to war, his anti-German sentiment incited him to call the French to sacrifice anything to triumph over Germany. Consequently, when Raymond Poincaré (French statesman, 1860-1934) called him to government in November 1917 as the conflict was at a critical stage, his only declaration to the French National Assembly was "I'm going to war!" Supported by a large parliamentary majority, he implemented a policy of public safety and castigated defeatists. To him, war could only lead to victory.

Following the Armistice, the French nicknamed him the "Father of Victory". It was therefore no surprise that he represented France at the peace talks aimed at regaining Alsace-Lorraine, safeguarding the border between France and Germany and securing war reparations from Germany. Clemenceau in fact hoped to force Germany to recognise the destruction inflicted on France. Nonetheless, he admitted that his country was not the only one that could boast of having played a part in the victory. Without its allies, France would have certainly been defeated. He therefore had to restrain himself and eventually accepted the creation of the League of Nations.

Elected as leader of the National Bloc (a centre-right coalition) in 1919, the supporters of *Action Française* (a far-right French political movement) reproached him for not being strict enough in the enforcement of the treaty.

In January 1920, he sought the presidency of the Republic, from where he hoped to monitor the implementation of peace treaties. But his defeat by Paul Deschanel (French statesman, 1855-1922) signalled the end of his political career. He spent the rest of his life largely alone, making the most of his free time for travelling and writing.

He died in Paris on 24 November 1929.

THOMAS WOODROW WILSON, THE IDEALIST

Picture of Thomas Woodrow Wilson.

Born in 1856, Thomas Woodrow Wilson was elected to the White House in 1912. A true pacifist, he proclaimed the United States' neutrality in 1914, thus limiting their involvement in the war to international cooperation.

But faced with the submarine war that Germany declared on the US in January 1917, he could no longer stay silent and had his country join the war in April. Wilson saw it as the opportunity to convert the world to democracy. On 18 November 1918, when he announced that he would be attending the peace talks, everyone was stunned. No president in office had ever previously represented the United States abroad.

When he arrived in Paris on 14 December, he tried to ensure that the peace treaty would be signed without any annexations. Wilson, in fact, wanted Germany to regain its powerful position without too much frustration, so that peace would be guaranteed in the long term. But Clemenceau did not share this opinion. The Frenchman believed that the creation of a buffer state (Territory of the Saar Basin and the Ruhr), occupied by the French army, was the condition for avoiding another war by reducing Germany's power. Unfortunately for Wilson, his ideals turned out to be incompatible with this aggressive European diplomacy.

Despite this initial failure, he was determined to fight for his convictions. The issue was now to get the Treaty of Versailles past Congress, particularly the creation of a League of Nations. In July 1919, he organised a propaganda campaign across the United States, which exhausted him. Immobilised by his declining health, he continued to fight from his bed, and demanded the adoption of the treaty in its current form, but the Senators refused to ratify it.

His policies, which aimed to pull the United States out of isolationism, were not successful. In 1920, he sought a third term, but the Americans chose the Republican Warren G.

Harding (1865-1923), who offered a return to normal life after the war.

On 20 November 1919, Wilson received the Nobel Peace Prize for his actions during World War I. Two years later, he retired from the political scene and passed away on 3 February 1924 in Washington.

DAVID LLOYD GEORGE, THE BRITISH LION

Picture of David Lloyd George.

Born in 1863, Lloyd George dominated British political life between 1906 and 1922. Initially opposed to Great Britain joining the war, from 1915 he developed the weapons industries necessary to the war effort and supported the policy of great offensives, notably the Dardanelles Campaign.

In December 1916, he replaced Herbert Asquith (1852-1928) as Prime Minister and led Great Britain to victory in the war. Additionally, his position allowed him to negotiate with the Americans and the French in Paris.

While he initially believed that Germany should pay for the damages caused, he ended up adopting the same positions as Wilson. Convinced that they would regain some of their power, he insisted on the importance of not humiliating them, out of fear of losing an essential partner for Great Britain. As for the League of Nations, he saw a way of involving the United States in Europe's affairs. When he returned to London, he hastened to have the treaty ratified, for fear that the House of Commons or House of Lords would refuse it, at the risk of delaying essential reforms for the country's economic recovery.

In 1922, the carelessness of his anti-Turkish policy in the Chanak Crisis (September-October 1922) caused him to lose power. Once again leader of the Liberal opposition in the Commons, he witnessed the break-up of his party. Increasingly isolated on the British political scene, he nonetheless did not lose his influence. With the help of the economist John Maynard Keynes (1883-1946), he began a reform project to turn Great Britain into a welfare state.

The Chanak Crisis was the first major test of Lloyd George's foreign policy towards Turkey, led by Mustafa Kemal Atatürk (Turkish president, 1881-1938). In complete disregard of the Treaty of Sèvres, Turkish nationalist troops attacked the Greeks in Asia Minor and besieged the occupying British forces in the small seaport of Chanak during the summer of 1922. Afraid of seeing the Turks threaten the British army in Constantinople, Lloyd George ordered the military forces of the Dominions to send troops to show the Empire's solidarity facing Turkey. Kept relatively in the dark about these manoeuvres, Parliament stated that this policy was careless and called for the Prime Minister's resignation. But the crisis was eventually resolved thanks to French intervention, which led to the Armistice of Mudanya on 11 October 1922.

In the 1930s, Lloyd George found it difficult to take a position on the rise of the Nazi party. In 1936, he even went to Berlin to meet Hitler (German chancellor, 1889-1945), who was happy to greet "the man who had won the war". But two years later, the Anschluss (the annexation of Austria by Germany) caused him to assess the powerlessness of Neville Chamberlain's government concerning the Third Reich's military redeployment. In 1940, in the House of Commons, he gave a historic speech that would strip Chamberlain of his title as Prime Minister, to be immediately replaced by Winston Churchill. The latter offered Lloyd George a position in his Cabinet, but he refused.

He spent his last years defending the consolidation of the welfare state, which he himself had initiated, and called for a calculated peace negotiation with Germany after the Battle of Britain (August-October 1940).

He died on 26 March 1945 in London.

VITTORIO ORLANDO, THE SIDELINED VICTOR

Vittorio Orlando.

Born in Palermo in 1860, Vittorio Emanuele Orlando was a moderate liberal member of parliament. From 1897, he worked alongside the head of the Italian Council of State, Giovanni Giolitti (1842-1928), as the Minister of Education (1903-1905), then the Minister of Justice (1907-1909). Between 1914 and 1916, he was entrusted this ministry again in the government of Antonio Salandra (Italian politician, 1853-1931).

Following Italy's defeat at the Battle of Caporetto (24 October-9 November 1917), he led the formation of a national union guided by the idea of resistance. He developed the economy energetically and reinforced the country's military strength, which would ensure the defeat of the Austrians at the Battle of Vittorio Veneto (October 1918).

In 1919, he chaired the Paris Peace Conference to ensure that the stipulations of the 1915 Treaty of London, which stated that unredeemed land would be returned to Italy in exchange for its commitment to the forces of the Triple Entente, were being respected. But when the time came, the Allies refused to honour their commitment, fearing that Italy would become too powerful in the Mediterranean. At a dead end, Vittorio Orlando decided to send Italian troops to Antalya (Turkey) and station them around Smyrna (modern-day Izmir), to force the French and British to give him control of the port of Rijeka (Croatia) at the expense of Yugoslavia. But this manoeuvre weakened him, and he left the negotiating table on 19 June 1919.

When he returned to Rome, he was elected as leader of the Assembly. He quickly attracted much criticism from the

Italians, who reproached him for not having been able to act in the interests of the country among the Allies and therefore having failed to secure compensation for the sacrifices made during the war.

Italy at that moment experienced a serious crisis, which stirred opposition between the trade unions and members of management, brought together within the new National Fascist Party led by Mussolini (1883-1945). Although Orlando initially supported Mussolini, who obtained power by force, he ended up joining the opposition when the fascists assassinated the leader of the Socialist party, Giacomo Matteotti (1885-1924), on 10 June 1924.

From then on, he refused to compromise on anything with the fascist regime and became somewhat withdrawn, particularly on 4 June 1944 when Rome was liberated by American troops. This reserve saw him elected President of the Constituent Assembly of the New Italian Republic in June 1946. But his objections to the terms of the peace treaty signed between Italy and Austria led to his resignation in 1947. As compensation, he was elected to the Senate the following year and, among many others, ran for presidency of the Republic. But it was the Liberal Luigi Einaudi (1874-1961) who was eventually elected on 11 May 1948.

Vittorio Orlando died in Rome on 1 December 1952.

THE TREATY OF VERSAILLES

A WIDELY CRITICISED TREATY

The Treaty of Versailles has a bad reputation. It is generally held responsible for the rise of Nazism in Germany and the war that ensued. But it is often forgotten that the agreement was the result of a delicate compromise between the four Allied Powers to try to re-establish peace in the explosive context resulting from the First World War.

In 1918, the unexpected fall of the Austro-Hungarian, German and Ottoman Empires led to the emergence of new countries that expected security guarantees from the victors under the rules of the nation-state, inherited from the 19th century. The three heads of state knew that, to achieve this, they would have to work together as part of a coherent institution, tasked with fairly recognising the responsibilities of both the victors and the defeated countries, at the risk of prolonging the resentment stirred by the war.

THE NATIONALITY PROBLEM AT THE BEGINNING OF THE 20TH CENTURY

In the 19th century, the balance of power in Europe was arranged according to the model of the nation-state. The theoretical basis for this model of sovereignty particularly emphasised people's freedom to live in a community within a defined territory, under a government capable of representing them and protecting them from foreign attacks. The application of this national principle, originating from Enlightenment philosophy, led to three distinct movements:

- The unification of countries into coherent territorial and political entities. The unifications of Italy in 1859 and of Prussia in 1871 are the best examples of this.
- The formation of national communities aiming for ethnic homogeneity to protect themselves from foreign influences. This was the case in the Balkans, where Greece, Serbia and Romania tried to assert their sovereignty against the Austro-Hungarian and Russian Empires.
- The co-existence, within these states, of several ethnicities who were dominated by the cultural model of just one, claiming a historical right to occupy the land or to call theirs the pure bloodline.

When the Empires collapsed after 1918, it was understandable that the notion of nationalities was particularly difficult to respect within territories where ethnicities were so numerous and so closely interwoven.

THE ORGANISATION OF THE VICTORS' CONFERENCE

On 18 January 1919, the Paris Peace Conference was opened by Raymond Poincaré. During the event, the French capital became the centre of the world. No fewer than 27 countries were invited to the negotiation table. Notable guests included the Belgian King Albert I (1875-1934) and the Queen consort Marie of Romania (1875-1938) alongside Portuguese, Polish, Greek and Serb delegations.

On 29 March, the decision was taken to create a supreme council made up of the United States, France, Britain and Italy. Japan was also invited, but its participation was limited to the matter of its colonies in East Asia.

Contrary to what had been expected, not all the formerly warring nations could be found around the negotiating table. The main absent party on the Allied side was Russia. Following the revolution in 1917, Clemenceau preferred to keep them out of it, fearing the influence the Bolsheviks might have over the negotiations. As for Germany, its responsibility for the beginnings of the war excluded it from discussions.

As the Chairman, Clemenceau opted for a rational organisation of the conference to avoid the main parties responsible for the war exploiting differences of opinion between the victorious countries.

"THE GREATEST CRIME IN HISTORY"

In August 1914, the German army invaded Belgium and committed acts of violence on nearly 6500 civilians. Four years later, the French government promised to prosecute German war criminals in an international tribunal to hold them responsible for the acts they had committed. For Great Britain, which had not been invaded, the recognition of Germany's criminal responsibility also seemed essential.

On a visit to London in December, Clemenceau accused Wilhelm II of committing "the greatest crime in history" and joined Lloyd George in demanding the emperor's extradition.

The British Prime Minister thus suggested creating an international court made up of Allied judges, with the jurisdiction to rule on the fate of those who had been accused of violating human rights. But as President Wilson refused, defending the jurisdiction of national courts to rule on war criminals, a compromise had to be found. It was therefore decided that:

- The Allies had the right to publicly accuse Wilhelm II of "a supreme offence against international morality and the sanctity of treaties" (Article 227 of the treaty);
- Each state could judge war criminals in their respective courts, by virtue of the principal of exclusive responsibility.

On this basis, the three Allies submitted a list with the names of the 854 people they wanted to try to Germany. However, the lists seemed so incoherent that Germany refused to hand over the defendants. Therefore, under pressure from President Wilson, who was anxious to keep the authority of the German government intact, they were reduced. Following these changes, Germany agreed to try the people involved. But the trial of the criminals brought before the *Reichsgericht* in Leipzig, starting in May 1921, was something of a disappointment.

A HEAVY DEBT FOR GERMANY

In addition to its crimes, Germany's responsibility was fully brought to light when the negotiators introduced the notion of war reparations into the treaty. Recognised as the only party responsible for the damages caused to the Allies during the war, Germany was forced to pay them compensation (Article 231). This idea was important to Clemenceau, who insisted on introducing it into the Armistice protocol, as France had suffered the most damage.

He wanted to weaken Germany's position by demanding reparations from them, but also by forcing them to give up Alsace-Lorraine and their colonies in Asia and Africa. Its army was reduced to 100 000 men. For Lloyd George and Woodrow Wilson, these conditions were too severe. While Germany certainly had to pay the price for initiating the war, the application of the reparation clauses meant that they were demanding much more than Germany could pay. Lloyd George consequently wanted to guarantee safeguards instead, to allow Germany to regain its position in Europe.

THE PEOPLE'S RIGHT TO
SELF-DETERMINATION

From the very start of the conference, Germany's situation highlighted the need to legally recognise, the respective statuses of the new nations that had emerged from the collapse of the Central Powers. Unlike Clemenceau and Lloyd George, who wanted to make this balance subordinate to the rights of the victors, Wilson was the only one who took a different approach by suggesting the principle of people's right to self-determination. This policy, known as the 'Open Door Policy', had the advantage of ending the pointless territorial expansion at the origins of the war, by giving each nation its own area of economic influence within a common, secure market.

The president also tried to influence the traditional sense of European diplomacy by encouraging his French and British counterparts to incorporate a clause providing for the creation of a League of Nations, whose role would be to monitor the collective security of the states and their good economic relations – particularly with the United States. While Clemenceau and Lloyd George agreed to include this project in the treaty's preamble, Wilson nonetheless did not get everything he wanted. For the Europeans, the re-establishment of peace was conditional on demands of independence and on power ratios in strategic territories that the Allies often allocated in their own interests. This partial way of defining nations' rights led to several lively debates around the negotiating table.

Among the subjects debated, Polish independence was one of the issues that raised the most questions. As they had fought on their side during the war, the Allies wanted to reward Poland by honouring Wilson's 13th point, which promised to restore an "indisputably Polish" territory to them. But the matter became more complicated when it was time to establish the borders of the new state.

In June 1919, the Treaty of Versailles officially recognised Polish independence, which had been proclaimed several months earlier. Aiming to create a stable buffer state to prevent the extension of Soviet influence into Western Europe, the Allies set the borders following the former Russo-German front line of 1918. Poland thus gained the Western half of East Prussia and the rich mining territory of Posen. The Danzig corridor was also given by the Allied commission to Poland, thus enabling their access to the Baltic, but refusing to recognise the 1920 referendum that showed a preference for re-joining the Reich. This decision seriously compromised the balance of the Eastern borders, and in the end nobody was truly satisfied with the outline imposed by the Treaty of Versailles. This explosive situation led to a new conflict between Poland and Russia beginning in February 1919. It would only end in December 1922, with the foundation of the Union of Soviet Socialist Republics (USSR).

The Allies' concern of reorganising Europe around a weakened Germany for the benefit of their own supremacy led them to draft an unbalanced treaty in June 1919. It was marked with the seal of the victors and cut off from the reality of the people whose interests it was supposed to represent in international law. In such conditions, having Germany accept it was something of a challenge.

A TENSE SIGNATURE

The Germans struggled to ratify this treaty as it removed parts of their territory, limited their army and stripped them of their colonies. Faced with the Allies' refusal to negotiate, the Social Democratic government of Friedrich

Ebert (1871-1925) were far from pleased. But refusing would jeopardise peace and expose the country to foreign invasion – as the French Marshal Foch was claiming his readiness to storm Berlin if the situation worsened. Consequently, on 22 June 1919, the Reichstag eventually accepted the Allies' conditions, by 237 votes to 158.

Signing the Treaty of Versailles.

On 28 June 1919, the Hall of Mirrors, where the event was held, was filled with tables and chairs. The delegations of the 27 victorious states, as well as the generals and the many infantrymen – for whom seats were reserved – were eager to witness the signing of the peace treaty. A crowd from all over Paris was also present to cheer the three heroes of the day: Wilson, Lloyd George and Clemenceau.

At around 3pm, the two German ministers, Hermann Müller (1876-1931) and Johannes Bell (1868-1949) entered the Hall. The crowd gave them a rather less warm welcome, and they signed what they called the diktat of Versailles. There is little doubt that this signature would give Adolf Hitler one of his main arguments for getting the Nazi party into power.

A TREATY CHALLENGED

When the Treaty of Versailles was ratified in January 1920, no state was truly satisfied with it, and two of the three leaders who drafted it lost their power: Wilson was defeated by Warren Harding, while Clemenceau lost to Alexandre Millerand (1859-1943).

In the United States, the treaty was rejected by Congress, notably due to the impossibility of Europe paying back the debt to them that it had incurred during the offensive in October 1918. This crisis led not only to the end of Wilson's career, but also to the refusal of the United States to join the League of Nations.

In France, Clemenceau was dismissed for being unable to obtain all the reparations necessary to the country's restoration from Germany. Nonetheless, this did not stop the National Assembly from ratifying the treaty on 13 July 1920. The return of Poincaré, who was from Lorraine, to the forefront of politics allowed him to modify certain clauses of the Treaty of Versailles, by allowing France to occupy the Ruhr valley as a guarantee that their reparations would be paid.

Beyond the interests of the three main Allied countries, the agreement did not manage to resolve essential problems, such as the establishment of the Polish borders. These gaps paved the way for fierce nationalist campaigns. Thus, across Europe, the application of a poorly conceived idea of nationality allowed political demagogues to lay the groundwork for wars on the pretext national sovereignty.

IMPACT

THE FAILURE OF THE TREATY OF VERSAILLES

In many ways, the Treaty of Versailles turned out to be a failure. The reasons for this can be found in the organisation of the peace meetings, but also in the consequences that certain clauses had.

Firstly, excluding Russia and Germany from the negotiations heralded more of a settling of scores than a balanced peace agreement that would take into account the interests of two countries who were crucial to European balance. It was therefore a thirst for revenge that led the three main negotiators to make the defeated parties pay by proving themselves inflexible on their demands – particularly the reparations owed by Germany – and not leaving any room for negotiation.

It is also essential to note the importance given to the Allied Supreme Council in the implementation of the treaties, in contrast to the weak powers given to the League of Nations in its role as mediator. Additionally, the institutions established by the Treaty of Versailles strengthened France and Britain's control over their colonies.

THE LEAGUE OF NATIONS, AN INEFFICIENT INTERNATIONAL INSTITUTION

The treaties made the League of Nations a body for maintaining peace following the First World War. Its mission was to minimise the risks of war by resolving disagreements between states. However, the lack of supranational authorities made it subordinate to the interests of the Allied Supreme Council, and limited its powers during the interwar period. Nonetheless, recourse to mediation allowed the status of some strategical territories that they administered in the 1920s to be clarified on several occasions. Thus, the Treaty of Versailles stipulated, for example, that a referendum had to be organised in Upper Silesia to find out if the region wanted to be part of the Weimar Republic or the Republic of Poland. In 1922, the League of Nations was invited to resolve the matter and managed to have the division of the territory between the two countries accepted. In the same way, it was entrusted with the management of the Saarland for France and the Free City of Danzig for Poland until 1923.

Aside from this aspect, the League of Nations was merely a mediation body whose arbitration could be effective in quelling crises limited to precise territories. But its effectiveness remained very limited when Europe's stability was compromised by more dramatic conflicts. Thus, the most important matters remained in the hands of the Allied Supreme Council. Consequently, the League of Nations soon started to seem like an obedient tool for global reorganisation, dominated by the European vision.

A BREEDING GROUND FOR THE SECOND WORLD WAR

Despite some notable success, the League of Nations soon showed itself to be incapable of responding to the many provocations of the Axis powers (Germany, Italy and Japan) which led to the start of the Second World War (1939-1945).

In Germany, the treaty was immediately met with the anger of the general public, and riots broke out. To show their anger, the residents of Berlin burned the French flags they had taken in 1870 during the Franco-Prussian War so as to not have to give them back. The most radical German leaders took advantage of this context to try to stir up people's anger with speeches that emphasised the humiliation Germany had suffered. Among them, an army officer named Adolf Hitler took advantage of these sentiments to unite workers' groups within the National Socialist German Workers' Party (NSDAP) and motivated them to action by promising to reunite all the German minorities that had been separated from the country by the "traitors of Versailles" into an "immortal Reich". This policy manifested itself in Germany's military redeployment, which remilitarised the Rhineland and annexed, starting in 1938, the Sudetenland (Germans in Bohemia) and Austria, with the approval of Allied heads of state who had gathered in Munich for the occasion.

In 1933, the Reich left the League of Nations, soon followed by Japan and fascist Italy in 1937, who refused to see their foreign policy, followed at the expense of China and Ethiopia respectively, subject to its judgement.

The League's inability to handle German claims to the Free City of Danzig marked its definitive failure. This crisis eventually convinced Hitler to invade Poland, on 1 September 1939.

SELF-DETERMINATION, A 'LOADED' EXPRESSION

When the treaty was signed, the Allies decided to make the principle of people's right to self-determination the basis of the new states' legitimacy, a concept that they linked to a radical application of the rights of birth and descent. These principles were soon understood by various European regimes as a threat to their stability.

When a state derived its legitimacy from the consent of the population – perceived as a nation – the presence of other ethnic groups was perceived as a threat for those who believed in their right to occupy the land. It turned out to be difficult for the Allies to give around 60 million people a state which was their own, without reducing other groups to the rank of minorities. This was notably the case in the Balkans, where the reforming of states which were otherwise too small to be viable made it necessary to unite populations which were not linked by nationality. Thus, nearly 3.2 million Germans could be found in Czechoslovakia, out of a population of 13 million. This imbalance was dangerous, as it meant that this small, central-European state was at risk of subversion by imposing minorities. The annexation of the Sudetenland by the Reich in 1938 was a good example of this.

In other cases, refusal to assimilate to the dominant culture led to the expulsion of entire ethnic groups. Between 1922 and 1923, the Turks organised the deportation of Armenian and Greek populations in exchange for Turkish nationals during the conflict that set them against each other.

Many more examples could be cited, but it is clear that by associating nations' independence with the sole criteria of a common language and a territory with borders imposed by a treaty, the victors of Versailles incited the frustration of the populations, who continued to fight to defend borders and territories that everyone wanted to be ethnically homogeneous.

FRAGILE ECONOMIC RECONSTRUCTION

In November 1918, the war that had just come to its conclusion had left Europe in tatters. In four years, the continent's intensive mobilisation for war had seriously weakened its populations and led to significant material damages, valued in 1921 at nearly £4 billion for Belgium and the North of France alone.

The destruction due to the war led to a large budget deficit for many countries, and made Europe dependent on the United States, who became its creditor thanks to its economy that had been boosted by the war effort.

The conference was the opportunity for some states to organise a proper communications campaign to convince Washington to intervene in their economic recovery. Thus, on 18 June 1919, King Albert I of Belgium took advantage of Wilson's visit to show him the damages caused by the Germans in the towns of Ypres, Leuven and the industrial mining area of Charleroi. The news relayed these images of desolation to the United States, which allowed the establishment of an aid fund (the Commission for Relief in Belgium), which was necessary for the country's reconstruction.

The United States' economic involvement did not last long. Scared by Europe's debt, the three presidents, Warren G. Harding, Calvin Coolidge (1872-1933) and Herbert Hoover (1874-1964), revived the isolationism that had existed before the war, hoping to thus keep their country on the path of economic growth. But this policy would only make the global economy even more fragile, as European stock exchanges were already too dependent on the whims of Wall Street.

In this context of economic fragility, the Allies struggled to overcome their hatred towards Germany, which was at the source of much of the damage. While they unilaterally proclaimed the Reich's legal responsibility, Poincaré, who wanted to humiliate the Germans even further, entrusted the occupation of the coal basins in the Saarland and the Ruhr to the colonial troops of West Africa. This provocation was too much for Germany, and the population was outraged.

Realising the danger that the rise of resentment represented in Germany, the League of Nations arranged for them to pay their war debt back in instalments so that economic recovery might be possible. Initially, the move failed. Germany in fact suffered a serious financial crisis between 1919 and

1923, which forced it to stop paying war reparations altogether after 1924.

The situation deteriorated in 1929 following the Wall Street Crash which devastated European economies, apart from that of the Soviet Union which experienced unprecedented growth from 1928 thanks to the development of a planned state economy. In retaliation, several countries decided to preserve their stability by turning towards dictatorial regimes: Italy with fascism (1924), Germany with Nazism (1933) and Spain with Francoism (1936).

At the end of the 1930s, the only solution available to Europe to attempt to regain the principle of freedom for its people, so extensively defended in Versailles, was to get involved in a new world war.

SUMMARY

- At the end of the First World War, the 1919 Paris Peace Conference aimed to restore relations between states by weakening the power of the former Central Powers, essentially for the benefit of France and the United Kingdom.
- The peace treaty settled the fate of Germany and accused Wilhelm II and his accomplices of war crimes. As well as incurring an enormous debt, Germany lost an eighth of its territory and had its army limited. In the West, Alsace-Lorraine was given back to France, while in the East, Germany lost Upper Silesia to Poland and part of East Prussia to Lithuania.
- The treaty also tried to oversee the political transition of Austria-Hungary and Russia's former possessions to democratic regimes. But the very new nature of mass democracy, along with the forced coexistence of different national groups within borders imposed by the victors, made Central and Eastern Europe very unstable.
- Despite the severity of the treaty's terms, Germany and Russia recovered quickly and reformed themselves around authoritarian and ideological regimes that won over their populations.
- In Africa and the Middle East, the victors also furthered their interests by strengthening their hold over their colonies. Through the intermediary of the League of Nations, they reduced the countries of Africa and the Middle East to the status of mere protectorates whose mandates were mainly shared between France and Britain.

- Designed to re-establish peace, the Treaty of Versailles only managed to reorganise the world according to the power ratios of the winners of the First World War. The states' inability to give up a small amount of their sovereignty for the benefit of collective security explains the failure of the League of Nations to fulfil its role as a mediator when faced with the excessive frustration of the states, who continued to see war as a legitimate option for ridding themselves of the injustices incurred by the treaties. Thus, instead of guaranteeing peace, the Treaty of Versailles only led to "eternal war".

We want to hear from you!
Leave a comment on your online library
and share your favourite books on social media!

FURTHER READING

BIBLIOGRAPHY

- Audouin-Rouzeau, S. (2014) *Encyclopédie de la Grande Guerre*. Paris: Bayard.
- Becker, J.-J. (2002) *Le traité de Versailles*. Paris: PUF.
- Becker, J.-J. (2004) *La Grande Guerre*. Paris: PUF.
- Becker, J.-J. (2008) *Dictionnaire de la Grande Guerre*. Paris: André Versailles.
- Deperchin, A. (2014) L'application des traités. *Encyclopédie de la Grande Guerre*. Paris: Bayard. pp. 1019-1031.
- Deperchin, A. (2014) La conférence de la paix. *Encyclopédie de la Grande Guerre*. Paris: Bayard. pp. 993-1005.
- De Schaepdrijver, S. (2004) *La Belgique et la Première Guerre mondiale*. Amsterdam: Peter Lang.
- Duménil, A. (2014) Les ruptures de l'équilibre. *Encyclopédie de la Grande Guerre*. Paris: Bayard. pp. 907-923.
- Gaillard, J.-M. (2003) Versailles 1919 : la paix des vainqueurs. *Les Collections de l'Histoire*, 21, pp. 100-103.
- Horne, J. and Kramer, A. (2002) *German Atrocities, 1914: A History of Denial*. New Haven: Yale University Press.
- Krumeich, G. (2014) Les armistices. *Encyclopédie de la Grande Guerre*. Paris: Bayard. pp. 924-935.
- Le Maner, Y. (no date) L'offensive allemande du printemps 1918, la kaiserschlacht. *Chemins de mémoire*. [Online]. [Accessed 1 September 2014]. Available from: <http://www.cheminsdememoire-nordpasdecalais.

fr/lhistoire/batailles/loffensive-allemande-du-prin-temps-1918-la-kaiserschlacht.html>

- Le Maner, Y. (no date) L'offensive victorieuse des Alliés en août-novembre 1918. *Chemins de mémoire.* [Online]. [Accessed 1 September 2014]. Available from: <http://www.cheminsdememoire-nordpasdecalais.fr/lhistoire/batailles/loffensive-victorieuse-des-allies-aout-novembre-1918.html>
- MacMillan, M. (2007) *Paris 1919: Six Months That Changed the World.* New York: Random House.
- Mazower, M. (2000) *Dark Continent: Europe's Twentieth Century.* New York: Vintage Books.
- Mourre, M. (1996) *Dictionnaire encyclopédique d'Histoire.* Paris: Larousse-Bordas.
- Réseau Canopé. (no date) La détermination des gouvernements. *Pour mémoire. L'armistice du 11 novembre 1918.* [Online]. [Accessed 1 September 2014]. Available from: <http://www.cndp.fr/entrepot/index.php?id=28>
- Vantoura, E. (2000) *Le traité de Versailles.* Québec: Centre national de documentation pédagogique.
- Wallart, C. (no date) Libération et armistice. *Chemins de mémoire.* [Online]. [Accessed 1 September 2014]. Available from: <http://www.cheminsdememoire-nordpasdecalais.fr/lhistoire/le-nord-et-le-bassin-minier-sous-loccupation/liberation-et-armistice.html>
- Winter, J. (2014) *The Cambridge History of the First World War: Volume 2, The State.* Cambridge: Cambridge University Press.

ADDITIONAL SOURCES

- Andelman, D. A. (2014) *A Shattered Peace: Versailles 1919 and the Price We Pay Today*. New Jersey: Wiley.
- Bennett, E. M. and Graebner, N. A. (2014) *The Versailles Treaty and its Legacy: The Failure of the Wilsonian Vision*. Cambridge: Cambridge University Press.
- Neiberg, M. S. (2016) *The Treaty of Versailles: A Concise History*. Oxford: Oxford University Press.
- Ullrich, V. (2016) *Hitler: Ascent, 1889-1939*. Trans. Chase, J. New York: Alfred A. Knopf.

ICONOGRAPHIC SOURCES

- Assassination of Archduke Franz Ferdinand of Austria. © Le Petit Journal.
- President Wilson asking Congress to declare war on Germany. Royalty-free reproduction picture.
- Picture of Georges Clemenceau. Royalty-free reproduction picture.
- Picture of Thomas Woodrow Wilson. © Pach Brothers.
- Picture of David Lloyd George. © Library of Congress.
- Picture of Vittorio Orlando. Royalty-free reproduction picture.
- Signing the Treaty of Versailles. Royalty-free reproduction picture.

50MINUTES.com

IMPROVE YOUR GENERAL KNOWLEDGE
IN A BLINK OF AN EYE !

www.50minutes.com